IF YOU WERE A KID IN THE
Thirteen Colonies

BY WIL MARA • ILLUSTRATED BY LLUÍS FARRÉ

CHILDREN'S PRESS®

An Imprint of Scholastic Inc.

Content Consultant
James Marten, PhD, Professor and Chair, History Department, Marquette University

Photo credits ©: Courtesy of Mount Vernon Ladies' Association. Photograph by Mark Finkenstaedt; 11: Philip Scalia/ Alamy Images; 13: svf74/Shutterstock, Inc.; 15: Steve Helber/AP Images; 17: DeA Picture Library/The Granger Collection; 19: Museum of the City of New York, USA/Bridgeman Images; 21: EntropyWorkshop/Thinkstock; 23: Print Collector/Getty Images; 25: Jiang Hongyan/Shutterstock, Inc.; 27: National Archives and Records Administration.

Library of Congress Cataloging-in-Publication Data
Names: Mara, Wil, author. | Farré, Lluís, 1970– illustrator.
Title: If you were a kid in the thirteen colonies / by Wil Mara ; illustrated by Lluís Farré.
Description: New York, NY : Children's Press, an imprint of Scholastic Inc., 2016. | Series: If you were a kid | Includes bibliographical references and index.
Identifiers: LCCN 2016000617| ISBN 9780531219720 (library binding) | ISBN 9780531221693 (pbk.)
Subjects: LCSH: United States—Social life and customs—To 1775—Juvenile literature. | United States—History—Colonial period, ca.1600-1775—Juvenile literature. | Children—United States—History—17th century—Juvenile literature. | Children—United States—History—18th century—Juvenile literature.
Classification: LCC E188 .M35 2016 | DDC 973.2—dc23
LC record available at http://lccn.loc.gov/2016000617

All rights reserved. Published in 2017 by Children's Press, an imprint of Scholastic Inc.
Printed in the United States of America 113
SCHOLASTIC, CHILDREN'S PRESS, and associated logos are trademarks and/or registered trademarks of Scholastic Inc.

2 3 4 5 6 7 8 9 10 R 26 25 24 23 22 21 20 19 18 17
Scholastic Inc., 557 Broadway, New York, NY 10012.

TABLE OF CONTENTS

A Different Way of Life

During the 17th and 18th centuries, hundreds of thousands of people came from Europe to create **colonies** in North America. These colonies were built on land where Native American people had been living for hundreds of years. At first, there were no towns and cities for the new settlers to live in. They had to form new communities and build new homes. Imagine being a kid in one of the 13 American colonies. You would probably live on a farm. You might have recently moved from a faraway country. Creating a better life in America wasn't easy. However, the hard work paid off for many families as the colonies grew and grew.

Turn the page to get a closer look at what life was like for some of those families! You will see that life today is a lot different than it was in the past.

Meet Charlotte!

This is Charlotte Sheppard. Her grandparents sailed from England to America long before she was born. They built a successful farm that Charlotte's father now runs. Charlotte is calm and dependable. She is the oldest of five children. She often takes care of her brothers and sisters while her father is busy . . .

Meet Elijah!

This is Elijah Coth. He lives on a farm with his mother and father. The Coths share their land with two other Dutch families. They all came from Holland four years earlier. Since then, they have had trouble keeping food on the table. Elijah knows his parents have considered moving back to Europe. However, he doesn't want to leave. He does his best to remain cheerful through the most difficult times. He has even learned some English from his friend Charlotte . . .

It was a chilly afternoon in the winter of 1670. Charlotte was feeling overwhelmed. Her father had gone away for a few days to buy seeds for planting in the spring. Because her mother had died the previous year, Charlotte had to look after her siblings. There was also a big storm on the way. It was up to Charlotte to make sure everything was put away safely before it started.

GETTING BETTER

If you get sick today, you can easily visit a doctor. You can then go to the nearest pharmacy to buy medicine. In colonial times, it wasn't always this simple. Most colonists lived far from doctors. Many common treatments had not been invented yet. This meant a simple fever could lead to much more serious conditions, even death.

Medicine bottles from colonial times

As the storm started that night, Elijah and his parents huddled in their home. The winds seemed to be getting stronger every minute. They heard a mighty crack as a tree blew down. Then came the sound of splintering wood. The tree had crashed through the wall! Freezing wind and rain poured into the house.

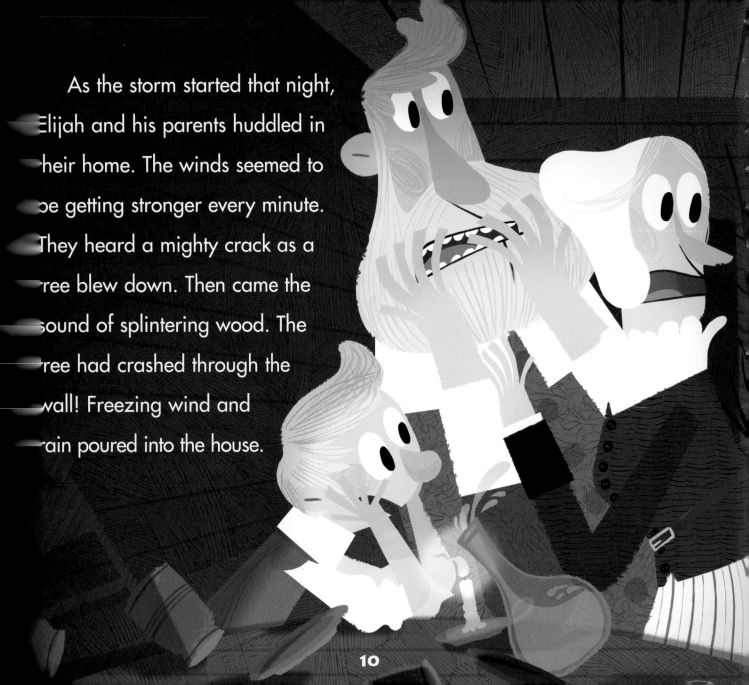

HOME SWEET HOME

Even today, a strong storm can cause major damage to houses. But this was a much bigger risk for many people in colonial times. **Rural** homes were often built by hand using wood from nearby trees. When your home was damaged, you had to fix it yourself. You would try to reuse damaged materials because they weren't easy to replace.

This New York house was built sometime around 1649 and still stands today.

The next morning, Charlotte went outside to see if the storm had damaged anything. Parts of the fence had been blown away. The barn was badly damaged. However, it could have been worse. Charlotte was relieved. Then she thought about the Coths. They lived down in the valley, where storms always seemed to hit harder.

COLONIAL FASHION

Today, you can choose from all kinds of clothes when you go shopping. In colonial times, you wouldn't have had so many options. Your family might have made their own clothes. They would be simple and made of strong materials. If they got a hole in them, you would repair them. And you would keep wearing them.

Sewing was an important skill for people in the colonies.

Charlotte was shocked when she arrived at the Dutch farm. The Coths' house had a hole in one wall. Another house had no roof. Worst of all, the storage building had been destroyed. The families' food supplies were mostly ruined.

"My father said we are going back to Holland," Elijah said sadly. "We have nothing left here."

"Come with me," Charlotte said. "I've got an idea!"

ARRIVING IN A SETTLED LAND

Though America was a new world to the colonists who sailed from Europe, it had already been home to Native American people for centuries. At first, the two groups were mostly friendly to each other. However, tensions grew as colonists took more land and spread deadly diseases. Over time, the conflict became violent. The Native Americans were forced into smaller and smaller areas of land.

English colonists traveled to America in ships like this one.

Charlotte took Elijah back to her house. She gathered her brothers and sisters and told them what had happened.

"We're going to bring them food and supplies," she said. "Our storehouses weren't damaged. Their need is greater than ours."

"Father is going to be angry when he gets back," said Charlotte's youngest sister. The others nodded.

"Let me worry about that," Charlotte replied.

MINGLING CULTURES

The colonies were home to people from many different **cultures**. Colonists did not only come from England and Holland. They also traveled from France, Germany, Italy, Scotland, Spain, and elsewhere. These people brought their music, recipes, clothing styles, and more to America. They also brought various objects from their homelands.

Their many ways of life blended together to create the America we know today.

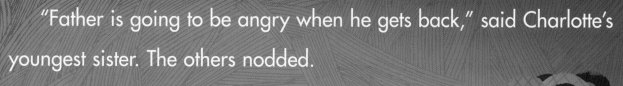

A traditional Dutch ceramic plate made in the 1600s

The Sheppards brought as much as they could carry to the Dutch families. Elijah's parents were confused about what was happening. Charlotte explained that they were welcome to all the supplies they needed. Elijah translated her words into Dutch. Elijah's parents were so grateful that they burst into tears.

A MIX OF LANGUAGES

European colonists spoke a variety of languages. They formed communities with other people from their home countries. This meant they could continue using their native languages. If you were a kid, you probably would have lived around people who spoke the same language as you. You might also have lived near groups of people who didn't understand your language.

An official colonial document written in Dutch

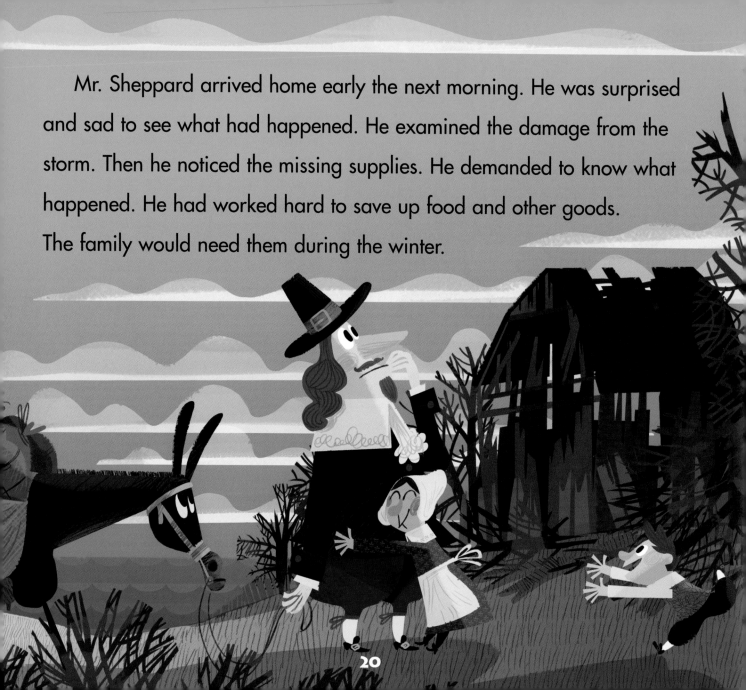

Mr. Sheppard arrived home early the next morning. He was surprised and sad to see what had happened. He examined the damage from the storm. Then he noticed the missing supplies. He demanded to know what happened. He had worked hard to save up food and other goods. The family would need them during the winter.

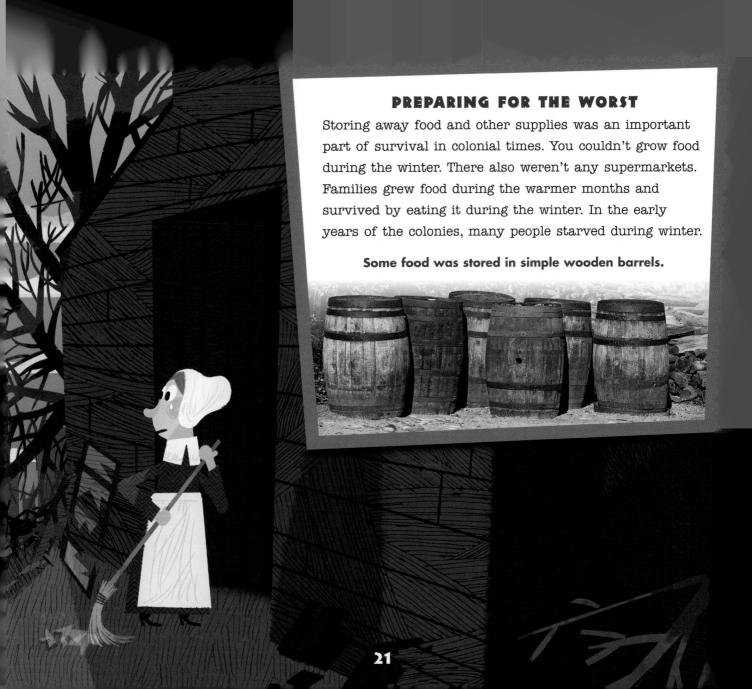

PREPARING FOR THE WORST

Storing away food and other supplies was an important part of survival in colonial times. You couldn't grow food during the winter. There also weren't any supermarkets. Families grew food during the warmer months and survived by eating it during the winter. In the early years of the colonies, many people starved during winter.

Some food was stored in simple wooden barrels.

At first, Charlotte thought about telling her father that a thief had stolen the supplies. She soon changed her mind. She told him the whole story.

"The Dutch families just needed those things more than we did," she finished. Mr. Sheppard sat quietly as he listened. Charlotte's siblings were afraid she would get in trouble. They stood by her. They told their father they had all agreed to give the supplies away.

YOUR NEIGHBOR, YOUR FRIEND

Colonists who lived far from towns or cities had to rely on their neighbors during emergencies. There were no ambulances, fire trucks, or police to help when something went wrong. But it wouldn't have mattered if those services had existed. There would have been no way to call them. Telephones had not been invented yet!

In colonial times, people could only communicate over long distances by writing letters.

Mr. Sheppard stared at his children. For a moment, they thought he was going to lose his temper. Then he suddenly gathered them together in a big hug.

"I'm proud of you all," he said. "Helping those people was the right thing to do. Now, come on. We've got a lot of work to do around here. Repairing the farm will not be easy, but it needs to be done."

24

KIDS HELPING OUT

Colonist children were expected to help out around the house every day. Sometimes these chores could be very hard and very tiring. If you were a boy, you might carry firewood, feed farm animals, or work in the fields. If you were a girl, you might knit, sew, cook, and clean. Most children had time to play each day, but not much.

Carrying firewood was hard work, but it was necessary for survival.

As Charlotte stepped outside, she was surprised to see Elijah. Behind him were the rest of the Dutch settlers. They were carrying tools, wood, and other building supplies.

"We're here to help you with the repairs!" Elijah told Charlotte.

Charlotte smiled at her friend. "Does that mean your family decided to stay?"

"I think it does," Elijah answered. "Come on, let's get to work."

FROM COLONIES TO STATES

By the end of the 1600s, Great Britain controlled all of the 13 colonies. Many colonists soon became unhappy with the British government. They decided to fight for **independence**. From 1775 to 1783, they battled Great Britain in the American Revolutionary War. After the war, the 13 colonies became the United States of America.

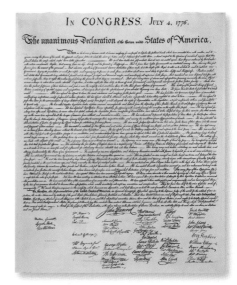

The colonies officially separated from Great Britain by issuing the Declaration of Independence in 1776.

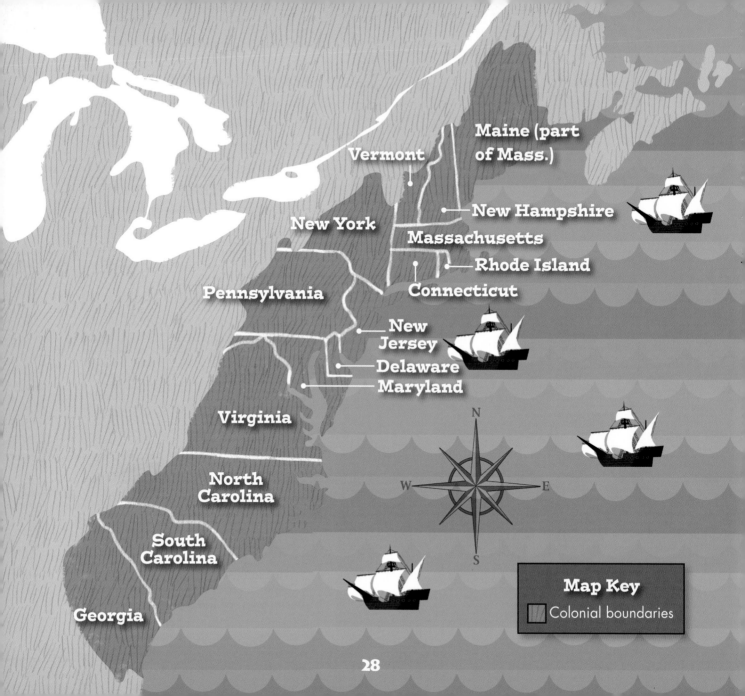

Vermont

Maine (part of Mass.)

New York

New Hampshire

Massachusetts

Rhode Island

Pennsylvania

Connecticut

New Jersey

Delaware

Maryland

Virginia

North Carolina

South Carolina

Georgia

N

W   E

S

Map Key

Colonial boundaries

Timeline

1607 Jamestown, the first permanent English settlement, is founded in Virginia near land that was home to the Wampanoag people.

1619 Enslaved African people are brought to British colonies in North America for the first time.

1620 The Pilgrims arrive in North America aboard the *Mayflower*.

1700 The population of settlers in the colonies is around 250,000.

1775 The population of settlers in the colonies is around 2,500,000.

1775 The American Revolutionary War begins.

Words to Know

colonies (KAH-luh-neez) territories that have been settled by people from another country and are controlled by that country

cultures (KUHL-churz) the ideas, customs, traditions, and ways of life of groups of people

independence (in-di-PEN-duhns) freedom from being controlled or affected by other people

rural (ROOR-uhl) of or having to do with the countryside, country life, or farming

Index

ABOUT THE AUTHOR

Wil Mara is a best-selling and award-winning author of more than 150 books, many of which are educational titles for children.

Visit this Scholastic Web site for more information about the Thirteen Colonies:

www.factsfornow.scholastic.com

Enter the keywords **Thirteen Colonies**

ABOUT THE ILLUSTRATOR

After illustrating more than 100 books over the past 20 years, Lluís Farré has drawn around 40 witches, 200 dragons, 500 princesses (and the corresponding princes), and more than 1,000 kids from different parts of the world and different moments in history. He lives in the coastal city of Barcelona, Spain.

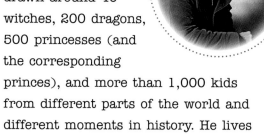